KNOCK KNOCK JOKES
MONKEY MADNESS

NICKY BIRD

FOLK LORE PUBLISHING

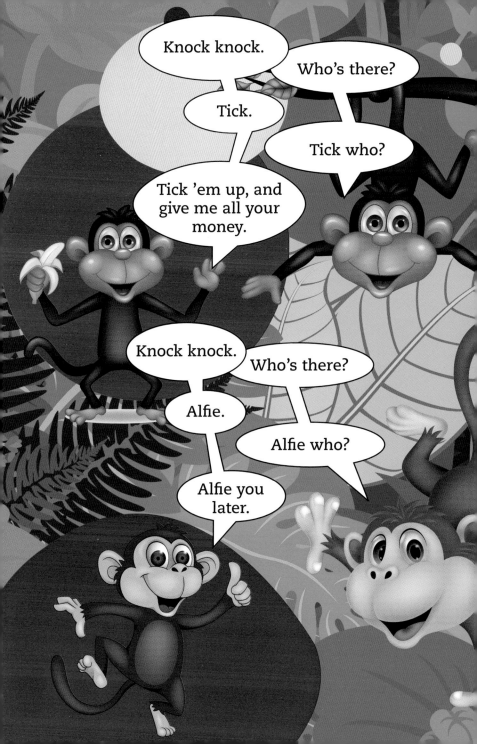

First printed in 2015 10 9 8 7 6 5 4 3 2 1

Printed in China

The Publisher: Folklore Publishing Ltd.
Website: www.folklorepublishing.com

Library and Archives Canada Cataloguing in Publication

Bird, Nicky, 1961–, author   Knock knock jokes : monkey madness / Nicky Bird.

ISBN 978-1-926677-98-9 (paperback)

  1. Knock-knock jokes. 2. Wit and humor, Juvenile. I. Title.

PN6231.K55B58   2016 jC818'.602   C2015-907835-0

Cover images: Front cover: Thinkstock: Tigatelu. *Back cover:* Thinkstock: Tigatelu.

Background images: Thinkstock: B-A-C-O, 6, 16, 26, 36, 46, 56; skellos, 2, 8, 10, 12, 18, 20, 28, 30, 38, 40, 48, 50, 58, 60; Yuriy Kozoriz, 4, 14, 24, 34, 44, 54.

Image credits: Thinkstock: Gabylya, 4, 10, 12, 13, 18, 19, 24, 34, 35, 42, 43, 52, 53, 57, 28, 29; IgorZakowski, 7, 14, 18, 23, 25, 27, 36, 40, 44, 49, 55, 58; Jorgenmac, 6–9, 11, 14, 15, 19, 22, 23, 25–27, 30, 31, 37, 40, 41, 45–47, 49, 54, 55, 58–60; liusa, 7, 14, 19, 23, 36, 37, 44, 49, 59; Tigatelu, 2–6, 8–18, 20–22, 24–48, 50–58, 61–63.

Produced with the assistance of the Government of Alberta, Alberta Media Fund.

Government

We acknowledge the financial support of the Government of Canada through the Canada Book Fund (CBF) for our publishing activities.

Canadian   Patrimoine
Heritage   canadien

PC: 30